a pock...

RHYME

Imagination for a new generation

2006 Poetry Competition for 7-11 year-olds

YoungWriters

GW01465030

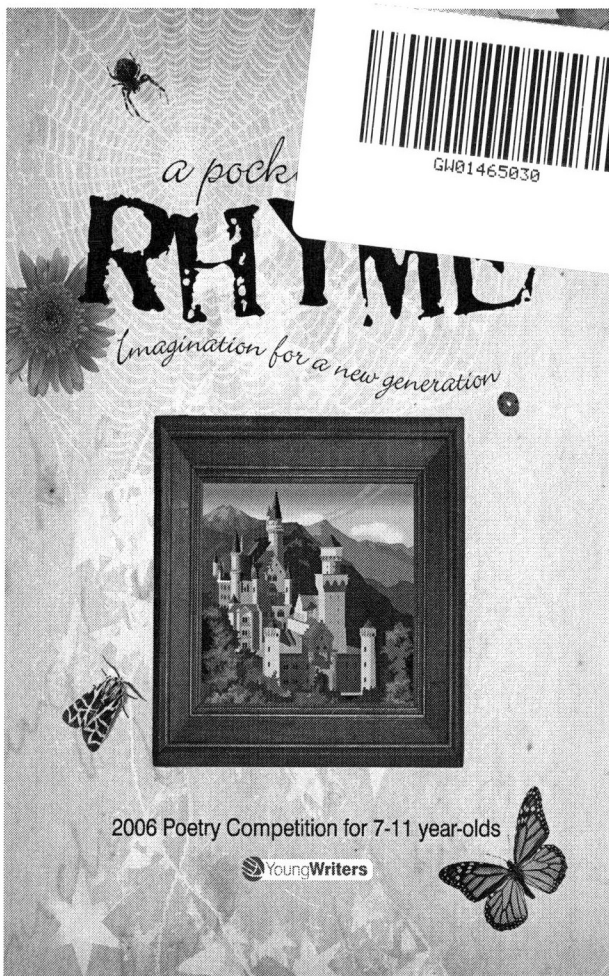

British Isles
Edited by Gemma Hearn

Young**Writers**

First published in Great Britain in 2006 by:
Young Writers
Remus House
Coltsfoot Drive
Peterborough
PE2 9JX
Telephone: 01733 890066
Website: www.youngwriters.co.uk

SB ISBN 1 84602 477 3

Foreword

Young Writers was established in 1991 and has been passionately devoted to the promotion of reading and writing in children and young adults ever since. The quest continues today. Young Writers remains as committed to the nurturing of poetic and literary talent as ever.

This year's Young Writers competition has proven as vibrant and dynamic as ever and we are delighted to present a showcase of the best poetry from across the UK and in some cases overseas. Each poem has been selected from a wealth of *A Pocketful Of Rhyme* entries before ultimately being published in this, our fourteenth primary school poetry series.

Once again, we have been supremely impressed by the overall quality of the entries we have received. The imagination, energy and creativity which has gone into each young writer's entry made choosing the poems a challenging and often difficult but ultimately hugely rewarding task - the general high standard of the work submitted ensured this opportunity to bring their poetry to a larger appreciative audience.

We sincerely hope you are pleased with this final collection and that you will enjoy *A Pocketful Of Rhyme British Isles* for many years to come.

Contents

Andreas Primary School, Andreas, Isle of Man

Lindsey Allen (8)	1
Ruby McCambridge (9)	1
Callum Kinrade (8)	2
Benjamin Jones (10)	2
Breeshey Moffatt	2
Ben Convery (9)	3
Aaron Sharples (8)	3
Alexander Jones (9)	3
Paige Lace (8)	4
Craig Beaumont (9)	4
Breeshey Evans (8)	4
Hannah Skillicorn (9)	5
Kate Teare	5
Charlie Morrey (8)	5
Katie Revill (8)	6
Bethan Cannell (8)	6
Francesca Pailor (9)	6
Jessica Davidson	7
Samual Robertson (9)	7
Kieran Cleator (9)	7
Charlotte Torr	8
Paige Perry (8)	8
Sophie Dobbie-Williams (9)	8
Callum Greaves	9
Kellie Rutter	9
Ffinlo Martin (8)	9
Megan Fielden (9)	10
Tara Lloyd-Davies (9)	10

Ballasalla Primary School, Ballasalla, Isle of Man

Danielle Oates (9)	10
Anna Watterson (10)	11
Andrew Corkill (11)	11
Lauren Gelling (11)	11
Kelly Firth (10)	12
Mason McLarney (10)	12
Abigail Jones (10)	13
Adam Young (11)	13

Zoe Beer (10)   14
Breeshey Mort (10)   14
Thomas Bott (11)   15
Eliza Faragher (9)   15
Billy Harris (11)   16
Alex Maitland (10)   16
Imogen Wild (10)   17
Craig Rodger (11)   17
Rohana Qureshi (10)   18
Jake Grimshaw (10)   18
Jack Garrett (10)   18
Makala John (9)   19
Lauren Jones (10)   19
Lauren Dean (9)   19
Paul Bott (9)   20
Siobhan Leonard (11)   20
Imogen Cannell (11)   21
Laura Beggs (11)   21

Castel Primary School, Castel, Guernsey
Katy Melhuish (10)   22
Eleni Falla (9)   23
Nicole Prevel (10)   24
Adam Stannard (10)   25
Tia Brown (11)   26
Clare Henry (9)   26

Grands Vaux Primary School, St Saviour, Jersey
Stephanie Vibert (11)   27
Amber Hopwood (11)   27
Sally Crago (11)   28
Ebony Vibert (11)   28

La Moye School, St Brelade, Jersey
Fraser Webb (10)   28
Jack McDermott (10)   29
Rose Laurent (10)   29
Callum Coote (11)   30
Jenna Bisson (10)   30
Hayley Bisson (10)   31

Rachel Lewis (10)	31
Luke Barrot (10)	32
Jordan Sewrey (10)	32
Tom Anderson (10)	33
Joseph Chadd (10)	33
Myles Bardin (11)	33
Laura Baker (11) & Eloise Prouten (10)	34
Danielle Costford (10)	35
Emily Aitchison (11)	36
Sarah Stokes (11)	36
Isley Wylie Le Greaves (11)	37
Abbey Le Main (10)	37
Robyn Laffoley (11)	38
Lauren Mollet (11)	38
Michelle Molloy (10)	39
Robyn James (10)	39
Nathan Hayes (11)	40
Joshua O'Donoghue (10)	40
Andrew Vallois (10)	41
Jack Hinton (11)	41
Katy Hughes (11)	42
Ben Gibson (10)	42
Kieran Sharman (10)	42
Kieran Kennedy (10)	43
Tom Chadd (10)	43
James Donnelly (11)	43
Jack Treliving (11)	44
Keiffer Davis (10)	45
Jamie Larbalestier (10)	45

Mont Nicolle Primary School, St Brelade, Jersey

Aiman Baghiani (8)	45
Bryony Harris (8) & Nicole Le Cuirot (9)	46
Shea Scott (9)	46
Hannah Taylor (9)	47
Eden Harrison (8)	47
Lauren Lowe (9)	48
Sean Durham-Waite (9)	48
Benjamin Carter (8)	48
Dominic Ball (8)	49
Phoebe Gould (9)	49

Claudia Barker (8)   49
Georgia Sharp (8)   50
Cameron O'Neill (8)   50
Sophie Young (8)   51
Max Taylor (8)   51
Cassandra Pickersgill (8)   52
Niamh Martin (9)   53
Scott McClurg (8)   53

Murray's Road Junior School, Douglas, Isle of Man
Henry Sayle (9)   53
Thomas Whitelegg (9)   54
Philippa Kennaugh (9)   54
Emily Rimmer (8)   54
Emily Brennan (9)   55
Molly Harding (8)   55
Emma Wilcox (10)   55
Katy Libreri (9)   56
Myriam Raso (9)   56
Jemima Morrow (10)   56
Rebecca Johnson (10)   57
Jack Berry (11)   57
Nicole Burns (8)   57
Jamie Kneen (7)   58
Ella Voysey (9)   58
Eleanor Goddard (9)   58
Eva Boyd (8)   59
Katie McKnight (7)   59
Courtney Marchbank (7)   59
Siobhan Fuller (8)   60
Fay Wilcox (8)   60
Max Fleurbaay (7)   61
Sam Greasley (8)   61
Caitlin Cowin (8)   62
Owen Phillips (8)   62
Sophie Cuthbert (9)   63
Kyle Logan (11)   63
India Halsall (9) & Bethanie Christian (8)   64
Kelly-Anne Hollingsworth (8)   64
Charlotte Percival (10)   64
James Collister (9)   65

Adam Smith (10)   65
Katie Banks (11)   65
Ruth Mellon (7)   66
Katherine Blenkinsop (9)   66

St John's School, St John, Jersey

Emilia Crocker (6)   66
Benjamin Tait (6)   67
Magdalena Thebault (7)   67
Hannah Couriard (9)   67
Kealan Bisson (8)   68
Hugh Percival (9)   68
Verity Stanier (8)   69
Hamish Morrison (6) & Luke Ryan (7)   69
Alexander Le Blancq (9)   70
Max Cornish (7)   70
Shane Galloway (9)   70
Áine Loynd (8)   71
Ben Jehan (9)   71
Jake Haslam (9) & Liam Baudin (10)   71
Aston Myatt (10)   72
Kelly McCullagh (10)   72
Catherine Rook (10)   73
Amy Condron-Dorey (10)   73
Eleisha Rice (9) & Molly Huelin (10)   74
Harry Lewis (8)   74
Jordan Stott (9)   74
Jack McGinney (10)   75
Corinne Figueira (9)   75
Scott Gallichan (8)   75
Ben Bidan (10)   76
Anya Beuzeval (9)   76
Bradley Le Feuvre (8)   76
Jayson Baudains (8)   77
Chloe McCabe (9)   77
Claire Le Cornu (9)   77
Philip Mitchell (10)   78
Robyn Nerac (9)   78
Alexander Touzel (10)   78
Jack Lewis (9)   79
Alex Watson (10)   79

George Queree (9)	79
Jessica Stamps (11)	80
Rikki Beuzeval (11)	80
Nadia Crocker (10)	81
Bradley Delap (10)	81
Emma Nelson (10)	82
Jarina Le Main (10)	82
Paige Therin (11)	83
Peter Rondel (10)	83

St Peter's Primary School, St Peter, Jersey

Matthew Palmer (9)	83
Sam Gorvel (8)	84
Amir Ben-Romdhane (9)	84
Emmanuelle Belligoi (8)	85
Alex De La Perrelle (9)	85
Sophie Wolstenholme (8)	86
Rebecca Knight (9)	87
Leo Loftsson (9)	87
Sophia Martins (8)	88
Abby McLaughlin (9)	88
Joshua Benest (8)	89
Kayleigh Nield (8)	89
Deborah Le Rendu (9)	90
Esther Le Ruez (9)	90
Daniel MacFarlane (9)	91
João Sousa (8)	91
Lauren Handscomb (9)	92
Ashley Knights (8)	92
Luke Oughton (9)	92
Daniel McMillan (9)	93
James Wall (9)	93
Bradley Le Couteur (8)	93
Rafael Pires (9)	94
Kai Walters (8)	94
Sophie Franckel (9)	95
Megan Ward (8)	95
Lisa Saout (9)	96

The Poems

Monkeys

Cheeky monkeys bouncing around,
Falling from trees to the ground.
Swinging from branch to branch of the trees,
Saying, 'Can I have another banana, please?'
Monkeys are the cheekiest pets,
But I still think they're the best.

Monkeys making noises like kettles,
When they're tired, every monkey settles.
All day helping each other,
Riding on the back of their mother.
Eating lots of food
And being in a happy mood.

Lindsey Allen (8)
Andreas Primary School, Andreas, Isle of Man

Crazy Family!

First there's my mum and dad,
Who are completely mad.
Then there's my sister, Lily,
Who is very silly.
I have a dog who's very dumb,
But really he's just a bit of fun.
We have another dog, she hates the vet,
She *really* hates our other pet!
I also have a cat,
He just sleeps on a mat,
And then there's me,
What a crazy family!

Ruby McCambridge (9)
Andreas Primary School, Andreas, Isle of Man

MX Racing

Over a jump, down a straight,
Round a corner, you're nearly there.
Hurry up, hurry up,
The others are behind you.
The chequered flag's not that far away,
Come on, you're there,
But don't be scared to go fast.
You have crossed the finish line,
You're there.

Callum Kinrade (8)
Andreas Primary School, Andreas, Isle of Man

Cats

C ats are furry
A nd very soft
T heir tails are very long
S ome are long-haired, some are short

R eally nice pets to have
U seful for catching mice
L ovely manners
E at up all their food (sometimes).

Benjamin Jones (10)
Andreas Primary School, Andreas, Isle of Man

Hedgehog

Hedgehog, bristly, spiky,
Bristled, spiked skin,
As quiet as a timid mouse,
Smells like the cold winter,
He tastes like slimy worms,
He feels like a spiked kitten,
Hedgehog - the spikiest but cutest creature
That could ever hibernate.

Breeshey Moffatt
Andreas Primary School, Andreas, Isle of Man

My Dog, Scooby

Black, fast, happy.
Seeing him look so black and run so fast.
Hearing him bark loudly.
Smelling him is gross.
He smells like an old banana.
Tastes like a bin.
Feels like a very smooth piece of paper.

Ben Convery (9)
Andreas Primary School, Andreas, Isle of Man

Tiger

Like an orange, soft, sparkling black striped layer of fur.
Softly padding across the wild stink of the forest.
The foul smell of dead flesh.
Like a leak of the crunchy, muddy forest.
It feels like soft, smooth, glistening fur.

Aaron Sharples (8)
Andreas Primary School, Andreas, Isle of Man

Killer Whale

Killer whale, blood, cursing mouth.
Black and white skin
And huge fins the size of lorry wheels.
Shimmers through the water
Searching for prey.
Stinks of flesh and blood,
But its smooth skin feels like fish scales.

Alexander Jones (9)
Andreas Primary School, Andreas, Isle of Man

Horses

Horses, sweet, fast,
As brown as the bark of a tree.
Galloping as fast as the wind.
Horses smell like golden hay,
They taste of the wild west.
Horses feel like teddy bears,
Horses are sweet animals.

Paige Lace (8)
Andreas Primary School, Andreas, Isle of Man

Monsters

A werewolf can't die,
A vampire can fly,
A monster can bite off your head,
No wonder I'm scared,
Cos the noise I've just heard,
Means that they're all hiding under my bed.
Aaargh!

Craig Beaumont (9)
Andreas Primary School, Andreas, Isle of Man

The Penguin

Penguin, cute, cuddly,
Seeing her waddle to and fro,
Hearing her feet in the snow,
Smelling her scent of slimy fish,
Tasting of an old food dish,
Feeling of a soft baby's sole,
She lives in the South Pole.
You will find her sliding, tummy first
As queen of the snow!

Breeshey Evans (8)
Andreas Primary School, Andreas, Isle of Man

Dolphins

Dolphins, graceful, cute.
Dolphins blue and grey
With a blubber coat,
With that nice, kind voice they have.
They smell like the fish in the sea,
They taste the scrummy fish.
They feel like my sister,
When she was first born.

Hannah Skillicorn (9)
Andreas Primary School, Andreas, Isle of Man

My Dog, Flin

I love Flin,
He raids the bin,
I take him on walks,
I think he talks.
His silky, wet nose,
Is as wet as a hose.
His ears prick up,
When he hears the whistle.
You should have heard him howl,
When he stood on a thistle!

Kate Teare
Andreas Primary School, Andreas, Isle of Man

Lion

Lion, furry, deadly.
Golden, furry, giant paws
Enormous roar through the world
Smells of dirt and flesh
The taste of cubs and the exotic jungle too
But his fur is as soft as grass
And he purrs like an overgrown cat.

Charlie Morrey (8)
Andreas Primary School, Andreas, Isle of Man

Winter

The trees are moving in the breeze,
I feel like I'm going to sneeze.
The cold wind blows,
The snow falls on my toes.
The playground has frozen,
Beneath my nose.
My house is covered in icicles,
I wish I could go on my bicycle.

Katie Revill (8)
Andreas Primary School, Andreas, Isle of Man

Dogs

A black, shiny nose,
A fluffy tail,
Fluffy hair
And a mouth that chews the mail.

Two floppy ears,
Here for you and I,
Come in different types,
What animal am I?

Bethan Cannell (8)
Andreas Primary School, Andreas, Isle of Man

Pony

Pony, brown, dark, sleek coat,
Clatter of hooves in the grey stable yard,
Rich smell of the cosy stables,
The taste of golden, crunchy oats on his pink tongue,
Feels like silky hair that's just been washed,
But he's very energetic going over jumps.

The beautiful pony,
King of the sweet-smelling stables.

Francesca Pailor (9)
Andreas Primary School, Andreas, Isle of Man

Horses

Horses, running with lightning,
Dark brown, fluffy, sleek coat,
Hard stamping on the hard, green grass,
Smells of wild blueberries on its tongue,
Feels like a woolly carpet,
It is soft and cuddly and it neighs like a little kitten.

Jessica Davidson
Andreas Primary School, Andreas, Isle of Man

Elephant

Grey, gigantic, a long water gun.
Grey as a stormy, cloudy day.
Huge feet stamping through the jungle.
Smells like golden, crispy leaves.
The taste of a dead snake.
Feels like a man's long, hairy legs.
The king of all beasts.

Samual Robertson (9)
Andreas Primary School, Andreas, Isle of Man

Cheetah

Big, furious, fast cat.
Hearing the paws looking for prey.
Smelling blood and torn skin.
The exotic taste of the wild jungle on his tongue.
But his glistening black and gold fur,
Feels like a soft, furry kitten.

Kieran Cleator (9)
Andreas Primary School, Andreas, Isle of Man

Horses

Horses running, wild and fast,
Brown, beautiful, pretty and spotty.
As cute as can be.
Muffled, loud trotting in the field,
Stamping on the grass.
Smells of food and horse mud.
The taste of fresh grass,
They feel soft and fluffy as can be.

Charlotte Torr
Andreas Primary School, Andreas, Isle of Man

Cat

Cat, furry, playful.
Seeing black, furry, playful cat.
Hearing soft purring noises.
Smells of cotton wool.
Tastes of cat food.
Feels so soft, you can hug them.

Paige Perry (8)
Andreas Primary School, Andreas, Isle of Man

Penguin

Black and white, like an old movie,
The penguins squeaking in the snow,
Feel like soft cotton wool,
Like ice and snow,
Like fresh fish.

Penguin, champion swimmer of the Arctic.

Sophie Dobbie-Williams (9)
Andreas Primary School, Andreas, Isle of Man

Cheetah

Cheetah, sly, mean.
Sparkly like a silky dress.
It purrs like a kitten searching for prey.
Of all the bloodthirsty animals in the grassland,
There's only one I know the best.
Cunning like a lion and soft like a mat,
The cheetah.

Callum Greaves
Andreas Primary School, Andreas, Isle of Man

My Family

First there are mum and dad
Who are completely cool
And don't forget my brother, Adam
Who is not cool like me.
I have a dog who is crazy
And a cat who is fat
And some fish.

Kellie Rutter
Andreas Primary School, Andreas, Isle of Man

The Cunning Lion

Lion, majestic, vicious.
Golden, glimmering mane and soft, gold coat,
The roar can be heard for many miles,
The smell of rotten meat,
The taste of desert and jungle,
His fur as soft and sleek as silk,
But in his heart he's an overgrown pussycat.

Ffinlo Martin (8)
Andreas Primary School, Andreas, Isle of Man

Ponies

Loveable, bearable, unstoppable,
I have a pony called Barney.
He has a beautiful, wavy mane and tail.
When he comes to me,
He makes a lovely, swift galloping rhythm.
It's like music.
My sister has to warn me not to go to sleep,
Because it's like a lullaby.
He's really cute and fluffy.
I don't know what I'd do without him.

Megan Fielden (9)
Andreas Primary School, Andreas, Isle of Man

My Dog

I like dogs with floppy ears,
My dog died in tears,
She got run over by a car,
She didn't get very far,
Before she died,
I heard her cry
And I said goodbye.

Tara Lloyd-Davies (9)
Andreas Primary School, Andreas, Isle of Man

Dogs

Dogs are cute,
Dogs are small
And when dogs are asleep,
They are like big, fluffy balls,
Dogs will always be my favourite pets.

Danielle Oates (9)
Ballasalla Primary School, Ballasalla, Isle of Man

Young Writers - A Pocketful Of Rhyme British Isles

A Dark Night

It smells like a mad, black volcano always bubbling all through
the night,
It feels like a damp, spooky, small, wet cave with bats flying in and out,
Darkness sounds like water dripping off the ceiling onto the floor of
a dark mine
And looks like a patch of black mist rolling into a dark night.
So next time when you are walking through the night,
Watch out for the creatures that might be in sight.

Anna Watterson (10)
Ballasalla Primary School, Ballasalla, Isle of Man

My Worst Nightmare

Darkness is a wild nightmare,
Where the Devil takes you into his lair.
Don't go in there if you dare,
You will die, but the Devil won't care.

The smell of the burned people's bones,
If you were caught, you would be all alone.
In the dark, with the Devil's eyes,
You would be easily seen.

Andrew Corkill (11)
Ballasalla Primary School, Ballasalla, Isle of Man

What Makes You Feel Happy?

When the sun shines on a rainy day,
And when I'm with my family,
When I enjoy myself,
And when I make people smile,
When I play with my friends,
And when I help other people.

What makes you feel happy?

Lauren Gelling (11)
Ballasalla Primary School, Ballasalla, Isle of Man

The Thing That Overrules My Heart

It's that something that makes our hearts
Pound with deep sympathy,
It's that thing that binds two souls together
With affection,
It smells of all things happy and warm,
It tastes of creamy caramels and chocolates,
It looks like nothing anyone has ever seen,
Like a glow,
It sounds like a drumming heart of life,
It reminds me of warm hugs,
My family and friends,
It is, and always will be, the most powerful thing,
Love can come in small and happy packages
And will always be there!

Kelly Firth (10)
Ballasalla Primary School, Ballasalla, Isle of Man

An Unpleasant Experience

Hunger smells like a fantastically favourite sweet,
It feels like an aching, bone-breaking body twister.
Tasting like an endless joy of magnificent food,
This is what hunger is about.

Hunger sounds like a screeching of pain,
Hunger reminds me of a nice, big, juicy steak.
Looking like a brightly wrapped present,
This is what hunger is about.

Hunger is a burning soul,
Hunger served in plate or bowl.
But it follows you all around,
This is what hunger is about.

Mason McLarney (10)
Ballasalla Primary School, Ballasalla, Isle of Man

Hate

Fifteen times I told my mum
I hate curry!
'Don't give me curry tonight, Mum,
I hate curry!
It makes my tongue fizz and burn,
I need fifteen glasses of water,
I hate curry!'

Squeezed tomato paste,
Looks like blood,
Spicy smells,
Disgusting,
I hate curry!

I can feel my face go red,
I screw my eyes up tight,
I don't want to hear Mum say,
'It's curry tonight!'
I hate curry!

Abigail Jones (10)
Ballasalla Primary School, Ballasalla, Isle of Man

Laugh Out Loud

A burning fire spreading down a path,
A summer giggle fighting to get out,
A relaxing liquid drink in the bath,
An exhilarating disease that makes you shout.

An invisible gas in an empty room,
A wild animal inside your soul,
An explosive bomb that makes you go *boom,*
The start of a fire loaded with coal,
These are all laughter to me.

Adam Young (11)
Ballasalla Primary School, Ballasalla, Isle of Man

The Night Sky

Stars like silver diamonds in the sky
Roads are like ribbons with a cold, icy chill.

Cars are like monsters on the roads
The moon is like a glowing rock with a cold and icy snowy shock.

Trees are whispering shadows
Plants are like waving people looking at the top of the church steeple.

Sheep are like clouds upon the hill
Cows are like splodges, brown and red, now it is time for their bed.

Children are like robots when mother says it's time for bed
Mums are like machines drinking coffee and eating fudge toffee.

Now it's time to turn off the light, goodnight, sleep tight
Don't let the bed bugs bite . . .
Right!
Turn off the light!

Zoe Beer (10)
Ballasalla Primary School, Ballasalla, Isle of Man

The Blackness Around Us

It is a being that wraps around the sun to make it disappear,
It smells old and musty as it weaves through the trees.
It tastes of liquorice as it hides in shadows,
It looks like a blanket has been thrown over the world.

It is the sound of water gently trickling over the Earth,
It reminds me of a panther creeping through the shadows.
Not being seen,
Not being seen at all.
In the blackness around us.

Breeshey Mort (10)
Ballasalla Primary School, Ballasalla, Isle of Man

Pursued

Running through that dark, lonely wood,
I stopped, my heart pounding. I stood in the mud.
I listened . . . cracking and snapping coming my way.
I spun round, cold sweat dripping on the floor. Why did I pay?
I ran fast and hard, tasting blood within my mouth.
The darkness as pitch.
I dropped suddenly into a deep, muddy ditch.
My pursuer stopped. I held my breath.
How did I get myself into this mess?
The darkness was calming.
The silence was soothing.
My pursuer left.
I accepted the sleep.

Thomas Bott (11)
Ballasalla Primary School, Ballasalla, Isle of Man

Activities

Hop, hop, hop
Jump higher and higher
Reach up to the sky

Stretch, loosen up
Get ready to run
On your marks
Get set
Go
Run as fast as you can

Listen to the DJs
Playing a tune
Find your partner
Dance, dance, dance
Around the room.

Eliza Faragher (9)
Ballasalla Primary School, Ballasalla, Isle of Man

The Dark, Freaky Castle

It's like being in the garden on a frosty Sunday morning,
Like the empty castle dungeon,
And the only thing in sight are the black, bare walls,
Beneath the grounds of the great castle.

It's like being in a graveyard late at night
And lying in your bed where the only thing you can hear
Is the clock ticking,
Until it's finally time to get up.

That's what it brings you.

Billy Harris (11)
Ballasalla Primary School, Ballasalla, Isle of Man

Going Across The Sea

Wander across that moonlit place
Where it's calm and smooth
Like a walk in space
Ponder where the star takes you
No early morning roosters coo.

Learn about the sea creatures
Nothing barks, wails or purrs
Just the dancing life underwater
There's mum, dad, son and daughter.

So that's all about the sea
It's like unlocking things
With a big black key.

Alex Maitland (10)
Ballasalla Primary School, Ballasalla, Isle of Man

Dog Show Jumping

Dogs bouncing about,
With leads and without.
1, 2, 3 - go . . . over the single jump and over the double,
Into the tunnel and out the other side,
Over to the weaving posts, *in, out, in, out, in out,*
Round to the see-saw, *up, up, up, down, down, down,*
Run, run, run, to the last jumps,
Over the single and over the double,
Time for the results.
The Dalmatian came third, Labrador second
And you came first!

Imogen Wild (10)
Ballasalla Primary School, Ballasalla, Isle of Man

Nightmare

Death in the air,
Horrible moments,
A demon's glare,
A devil's burn,
A walk in the woods,
Fear and cower,
A dead bat's fur,
A ghost lingering,
Not a whisper,
Not a mouse,
A spider's crawl,
A horrible night,
Ash in your mouth,
Close to death,
No freedom.

Craig Rodger (11)
Ballasalla Primary School, Ballasalla, Isle of Man

What Is Fun?

Fun is doing something new
It feels like a cuddly creature cuddling you
It's like a crowded room
It's waiting to be let outside
It's like you're on a long ride
You never want it to end
It's laughter all around
Always try and find a way to have fun
Fun is having a good time.

Rohana Qureshi (10)
Ballasalla Primary School, Ballasalla, Isle of Man

Fear

Fear is pitch-black, dark and terrifying.
Fear smells like a pig's pen and a horse's stable,
The headless horseman's head.
A dying yeller, that's what fear sounds like.
Steel, stone and brick, that's what fear tastes like.
The Devil himself, that's what fear looks like.
Fear is falling off the biggest building in the world.

Jake Grimshaw (10)
Ballasalla Primary School, Ballasalla, Isle of Man

Hunger Pangs

Hunger is waiting for a Christmas dinner,
Hunger is your stomach swelling up,
It smells like a big, beefy steak,
And it tastes like a big, juicy lollipop.

Hunger looks like a table ready for a feast,
Hunger sounds like a cow chewing the cud,
It reminds me of hot soup on a winter's day,
What does hunger remind you of?

Jack Garrett (10)
Ballasalla Primary School, Ballasalla, Isle of Man

Kitten Poem

Cats are cute, cats are small,
Have you seen the kitty-cat on the floor?
You know they're sweet, you know they're small,
Have you seen your kitty-cat on the floor?
Cats have kittens and kitten have colour,
Have you seen the kitty-cat on the floor?
Some kittens are boys, some kittens are girls,
Have you seen the kitty-cat on the floor?

Makala John (9)
Ballasalla Primary School, Ballasalla, Isle of Man

Kittens

Kittens are cuddly,
Kittens are sweet,
As they roll on the carpet
With little fluffy feet.

Kittens are furry,
Kittens can eat,
But kittens in the garden,
Were never meant to meet.

Lauren Jones (10)
Ballasalla Primary School, Ballasalla, Isle of Man

The Lily Pond

Splish, splash, like a frog,
Flip, flap, like a fish,
Quack, quack, like a duck
On the lily pond.

Lilies floating like the ducks,
Weeds swaying like waving hands,
And trees are blowing,
Near and on the lily pond.

Lauren Dean (9)
Ballasalla Primary School, Ballasalla, Isle of Man

Eagle Flying

When an eagle flies,
Something could be about to die.
Mouse or fish?
No one will know the eagle's wish,
And when he is in his lair,
All his children will be there,
Ready for their night-time meal,
But tomorrow only pain is what they will feel,
For their father has been shot,
By men who kill for fun.

Paul Bott (9)
Ballasalla Primary School, Ballasalla, Isle of Man

Creeping Around In The Dark

Fear is sneaking around in the dark,
Shouting and screaming out in the park,
It is waiting and making strange noises and sounds,
Crashing around in the garden and house.

A huge, scary monster jumping around and around,
Waving his arms and shouting out, *'Boo!'*
Hiding in boxes and then leaping out,
Scaring small children and making them jump.

Siobhan Leonard (11)
Ballasalla Primary School, Ballasalla, Isle of Man

Tangled In The Tomb Of Fear

Tangled in the tomb of fear,
Blood is on the wall, a smear.
Mummies scream, in a team,
A misty ghost, around a post.

Tangled in the tomb of fear,
Run for it, there's something near.
Haunted coffins, wound in bobbins,
Chopped off heads, hung in sheds!
Aaargh!

Imogen Cannell (11)
Ballasalla Primary School, Ballasalla, Isle of Man

Shining Joy

It burns in your eyes
And makes your stomach laugh.
It looks amazing with its shining colours,
It always says hello.

It is bright, like yellow,
It tastes like a big, juicy apple,
It sounds like a gigantic eruption.
Happiness reminds me to have some fun.
What does happiness remind you of?

Laura Beggs (11)
Ballasalla Primary School, Ballasalla, Isle of Man

Magic Box

(Based on 'Magic Box' by Kit Wright)

I will put in the box . . .

A sample of the gold, swirling sands of the finest blends,
A shining sunset sailing down with sorrow,
The glowing gulls gliding past,

I will put in the box . . .

A child telling an adult off as their voices echo into the night,
A mouse chasing a cat into a dusky, dull awakening,
The pant of a dog with wild legs as it runs through a glimmering
green forest.

I will put in the box . . .

A rageful polar bear that is feeling destructive,
The sinful cry of a T-rex as it tears through houses like a pair of
scissors through paper,
The innocent chirp of a glowing, gold canary perching on a branch
in front of the swirling sun.

I will put in the box . . .

A shimmering silver pen shielding sunlight,
An ink pen with flowing colours and a sharp nib,
And a silky silver wrap to secure the warmth.

I will end my box with a fantastic surprise . . .

All the peace and love in the world combined together to make a
huge heart of gold.

Katy Melhuish (10)
Castel Primary School, Castel, Guernsey

Magic Box

(Based on 'Magic Box' by Kit Wright)

I will put in the box . . .

A world of wonder whooshed away by the water,
A cat chasing a dog,
A marvellous magician performing all the magic.

I will put in the box . . .

Glimmering gold gadgets growing in the garden,
A hamster running free,
A fish in a cage.

I will put in the box . . .

A king working for a servant,
A bunny catching a cat,
A baby telling her mum the bedtime story.

I will put in the box . . .

A snail slithering along the sandy soil,
An endangered donkey digging up dynamite,
Being on the sand the colour of the sun.

Last of all I will put in the box,
A big Dairy Milk chocolate fountain to share!

Eleni Falla (9)
Castel Primary School, Castel, Guernsey

Magic Box

(Based on 'Magic Box' by Kit Wright)

I will put in the box . . .

The shine of the rainbow-coloured T-shirt on a summer's morning,
The vibration of King Kong beating his chest,
The threat of a toenail tearing tomatoes.

I will put in the box . . .

A shiny snake slithering slowly,
A book with a cracked spine,
A breathtaking view from the London Eye.

I will put in the box . . .

Pointed teeth from the naked mole rat,
The thirteenth month,
The starfish in the sky and the star in the sea.

My box is covered in white, shimmering, see-through gems,
The glistening stardust sprinkled over the lid
With rainbow wishes in the corner,
Its hinges are the golden claws of the great lion.

Nicole Prevel (10)
Castel Primary School, Castel, Guernsey

Magic Box

(Based on 'Magic Box' by Kit Wright)

I will put in the box . . .
A shining, sandy beach on a summer morning,
A brilliantly baked blackberry pie being sliced,
The raging roar of a razor-toothed dragon.

I will put in the box . . .
A volcano spurting ice,
A sheep with a goatie
And a goat looking sheepish.

I will put in the box . . .
A flowing ice river,
A snail with a speeding ticket,
A referee with a red card.

I shall fly in my box,
Over land and sea,
Then land on the highest mountain,
Crusted with snow.

Adam Stannard (10)
Castel Primary School, Castel, Guernsey

Socks

I have socks lilac, blue, much more too!
Dotted, striped,
Loose and tight,
I don't know what ones to wear to school in a fortnight!

My friend's sock is black
Like my fat cat,
My box of socks is red
So is my bed,
My brother's sock is grey
So is the day!
Outside is blue
So is my mum too!

I wonder what it is like to climb a rainbow
And my big toe.

Tia Brown (11)
Castel Primary School, Castel, Guernsey

The Magic Box

(Based on 'Magic Box' by Kit Wright)

I will put in the box . . .
A glimpse of a coloured T-shirt,
King Kong's vibration on his chest,
Threat of a toenail tearing tomatoes.

I will put in the box . . .
An oven
A chair with backache,
A book with a broken spine.

I will put in the box . . .
A breathtaking view of the London Eye,
Pyramids' treasure from a pharaoh,
Pointed teeth of a naked mole rat.

My box is fashioned with sparkle from a broken crystal.

Clare Henry (9)
Castel Primary School, Castel, Guernsey

Bonkey Wongos

Watch out,
Watch out,
Bonkey Wongos are about.

The leer,
They sneer,
They make you dream about fear.

They're mean,
They're green,
They're everywhere to be seen.

They fight,
At night,
Pretending they're solid knights.

They munch,
They crunch,
They will eat anyone for lunch.

Watch out,
Watch out,
Those Bonkey Wongos are out.

Stephanie Vibert (11)
Grands Vaux Primary School, St Saviour, Jersey

There Was A Young Carrot

There was a young carrot called Stu,
Who never knew what he should do.
He said he was hot,
As he went in a pot,
Oh, that poor young carrot called Stu.

Amber Hopwood (11)
Grands Vaux Primary School, St Saviour, Jersey

Aunty Pam

Aunty Pam loved her ham
She gave it to her nephew, Sam
He didn't really like it much
He much preferred to have some jam.

Poor old Sam, he hated ham
He nearly hated Aunty Pam
She made him eat up every bit
Instead of giving him strawberry jam.

He tried to tell her, he really did
But she didn't listen, he was just a kid
It nearly made him really sick
So in the end he told Uncle Sid.

Sally Crago (11)
Grands Vaux Primary School, St Saviour, Jersey

The Spud

There was a potato called Rew,
Who never had a clue what to do.
He got sliced into chips
And they fried all the bits,
Oh, that poor young potato called Rew.

Ebony Vibert (11)
Grands Vaux Primary School, St Saviour, Jersey

Lighthouse

I am the lighthouse
Stood up straight
Stuck in the rocks
As waves crash into my feet
My bones are the stairs going up
My eyes are the lights
Guiding ships to safety from danger.

Fraser Webb (10)
La Moye School, St Brelade, Jersey

The Blitz

Each night I unfairly bullied horrified families
Into hiding in dirty, dusty stations and filthy, stench-filled shelters.

With my long, dark cape,
I selfishly blocked out all sunlight from the world.

With my bare hands,
I pushed terrified children out of their destroyed city and into the
dirty country.

In the black and dead of night,
I demolished the homes of terrified families with my mighty fist.

With my harsh little finger,
I cruelly sent sirens screaming into the black of the night.

With my feet of fire,
I stood on the lives of innocent people and stole them.

I did all of this, for I am Blitz.

Jack McDermott (10)
La Moye School, St Brelade, Jersey

The Blitz

With the tip of my little finger,
I compressed and squished people's lives.

I pursued terrorised children away
To the security of the country.

I shattered everything and everyone
I made contact with.

With my scorching cigarette,
I flicked a black blanket of ash over the cities.

I dangled my black, dusty cape
Over the steamed up windows.

With my fiery balls of sweat,
I burned down cities.

Rose Laurent (10)
La Moye School, St Brelade, Jersey

The Blitz

With my great, cruel, powerful hands
I crushed people's houses.

I screamed my awful wail
In the dead of the night.

I kicked guiltless children
To the safety of the country.

I painted people's windows black
In the night.

Into the underground
I chased innocent people.

I murdered blameless people
With my exploding fist.

I am the Blitz!

Callum Coote (11)
La Moye School, St Brelade, Jersey

The Blitz

I covered people's windows
With the palm of my hand,
With my little finger,
I crushed people's houses,
Innocent people I murdered
With my enormous foot,
Children I kicked
On the train to the country,
I screeched
My deafening screech,
In the air raid shelters
I chased the terrified.

I am the Blitz.

Jenna Bisson (10)
La Moye School, St Brelade, Jersey

Young Writers - A Pocketful Of Rhyme British Isles

The Blitz!

With my burning, fiery tears,
I drowned innocent people.

With my cruelty,
I made innocent people's lives horrifying and distressing.

I draped my black cloak over the windows
To terrify the world.

To the safety of the country
I threw petrified children with my enormous, bold fist.

Every night I chased horrified people
Into air raid shelters.

In the black of the night
I screamed my deafening wails.

For I am the Blitz!

Hayley Bisson (10)
La Moye School, St Brelade, Jersey

The Blitz

My wails chase the people into the covering air raid shelters
From my friends, the bombs.

My crashes, terrify people running down the city road.
Away to the country, my evilness sent people.

As I come alone, I stamp on every house in sight,
As I drop and spread, I kill someone.

My hands pull out all the energy of light,
For I am the Blitz!

Rachel Lewis (10)
La Moye School, St Brelade, Jersey

The Blitz

With my mammoth feet,
I destroyed homes.

With my broomstick,
I hounded people into small shelters.

With my colossal hands,
I sprayed people's windows black.

With my duvet,
I covered the cities in darkness.

With the touch of my bare hand,
I destroyed people's lives.

I kicked children onto the train,
That took them to the bombless countryside.

Luke Barrot (10)
La Moye School, St Brelade, Jersey

The Blitz

I smacked many houses to pieces
With my gigantic, filthy fist.

I covered the city with darkness
With my massive head.

I screeched at the top of my voice
I was on my way.

With my humungous tears
I murdered innocent people.

I threw terrified children
Into the countryside.

Into dark tunnels
I chased frightened people.

For I am the Blitz!

Jordan Sewrey (10)
La Moye School, St Brelade, Jersey

The Blitz

I tossed terrified children away to the safety of the country,
I sat on horrified people retreating to the shelter,
With my bare, bloodstained and cold hands, I crushed
                                                innocent people,
I chucked people into the Underground while
I spat lethal bombs down to wreck the city,
To rush terrified people to the Underground, I blew my siren,
I poured over all the windows to make a blackout.

Tom Anderson (10)
La Moye School, St Brelade, Jersey

The Blitz

I blew people sky-high with my bloodstained hands.
Thousands of innocent people I murdered, using my sharp claws.
In total darkness, I left cities, flinging my long cloak behind me.
Stamping my humungous feet, I kicked people into the Underground.
To the safety of the country, I chased petrified children.
With my high-pitched voice, I warned people to head for the shelters.

For I am the Blitz!

Joseph Chadd (10)
La Moye School, St Brelade, Jersey

The Blitz

With my gigantic, blazing feet, I destroy houses,
All the way to the country, I flick innocent children,
With my fiery tears, I assassinate people,
To let them know I'm coming, I howl as loud as I can,
Into air raid shelters I chase innocent people,
All over terrified people's windows at night, I spit out black paint.

Myles Bardin (11)
La Moye School, St Brelade, Jersey

The Trouble With My Pets

My little kitten,
Is sometimes very lazy,
But most of the time,
She drives me crazy.

Suddenly, all big and sparkly,
My kitten grew a horn,
There shining on her head,
Just like a unicorn.

My tortoise has gone bonkers,
He bites the postman's arm,
I think the postman's scared of him,
As he sets off an alarm.

He eats dog food
And chases the horned cat,
But one day he hibernated,
Upon the kitchen mat.

My guinea pig has grown wings,
We taught him how to fly,
Yesterday he hit a tree
And then he said goodbye.

We had a nice big funeral
And buried him in a box,
Suddenly he rose up,
Turned out he had chickenpox.

But now . . .
Everyone's back to normal,
Except for Mum,
Who's acting a bit daft!

Laura Baker (11) & Eloise Prouten (10)
La Moye School, St Brelade, Jersey

The Blitz

I murdered everyone I could find
With my own bloody, bloodstained hands,
As I blew up homes
And everything I touched.

I covered the whole world
In devastating, gloomy darkness,
With my absolutely mountainous, huge cape
While terrifying everyone.

I laughed as spit came out of my mouth
Which was thunderbolts,
When everything and everyone
Was getting murdered.

I grabbed a child by the hair
And ripped it all out,
And then I shot him in the back
As his family were watching and couldn't do anything.

I went to all the concentration camps
And the labour camps and the death camps,
And made all the destruction
I could make.

I chased all of the families into the shelter,
And then threw loads of bombs
In the same place,
Until all of them were under rubble.

I am the Blitz!

Danielle Costford (10)
La Moye School, St Brelade, Jersey

The Blitz

As I watch with an evil glint in my eye,
Terrified children with their parents squeezing their hands
While rushing to the air raid shelters.

To the calm and peaceful countryside,
I chase young, frightened children without their parents.

With my exposed and sweaty hands,
I cover all the windows with blackout.

My frightening, icy feet
Leap on brick houses.

People scream
As I flick the awful wailing sound from the siren.

When innocents are sleeping,
I destroy with the fire from my mouth.

People surrender when I stomp and shout.
For I am the Blitz!

Emily Aitchison (11)
La Moye School, St Brelade, Jersey

Blitz

With my monstrous, evil bare feet, I demolished the town,
I destroyed the town with my humungous, reeking feet,
With an evil look from my eye, I terrified kids,
With my fire-breathing mouth, I burnt the city,
I hung my black cloak over the windows to alarm the city,
With a touch of my bare hands, angrily I took other people's lives,
Every night I chase terrified people into the air raid shelters.

Sarah Stokes (11)
La Moye School, St Brelade, Jersey

The Blitz

With my enormous feet
I murdered tiny, harmless people,

With my dirt-splattered hands
I flicked horrified children into the country,

I screeched at the top of my voice
That told people to rush into shelters,

With my tiny fingertips
I mashed every house in sight,

My colossal eyes shredded everything
That I saw with them,

With my grime-covered hands
I hurled buckets of black paint over every window,

> For I'm the *Blitz!*

Isley Wylie Le Greaves (11)
La Moye School, St Brelade, Jersey

The Blitz

With my unpleasantly cold hands
I murder the innocent people of London,

My gloomy, icy mind tells me to evacuate
But parts of me say no,

In the cold of night my stomach churns
As the sounds of sirens go off,

With night falling, I cover my windows
With my filthy, black sheet,

At the blare of a siren, my legs carry me far away
To a bomb shelter,

> *I am the Blitz!*

Abbey Le Main (10)
La Moye School, St Brelade, Jersey

The Blitz

With my humungous mouth,
I spat out fiery bombs to destroy the city beneath me.

I hung my giant black cloak
Over every house in the city.

I squealed so piercingly with my colossal-sized mouth,
That I nearly deafened people.

Into the air raid shelters,
I chased terrified people.

With the palm of my hand,
I packed children off to the country.

I devoured all the hope that remained,
For I am the Blitz!

Robyn Laffoley (11)
La Moye School, St Brelade, Jersey

The Blitz

My pointy, sharp nails
Screeched along the revolting window,

I grabbed people's houses
And threw them with anger,

With my bulky, disgusting feet,
I killed innocent people,

I shredded houses to pieces
With my colossal fists,

I banished the children
To the safety of the country,

With my little pinkie,
I made the city a misery.

Lauren Mollet (11)
La Moye School, St Brelade, Jersey

The Trouble With My Dad

My dad is a menace
He makes noises on the bus
Whenever we're around him
He blames it all on us

My dad is bonkers
He wears a lot of shorts
But when we have roast dinner
He eats like a horse

My dad is mad
He's bonkers to the max
He runs around the garden
Waving around an axe

My dad is very soppy
He cries in his sleep
But when he is happy
He acts like a sheep.

Michelle Molloy (10)
La Moye School, St Brelade, Jersey

Composed Upon Westminster Bridge September 3rd 2005

Earth has not anything to show more grotesque,
No living soul could pass by this sight,
Without the feeling of selfishness that led,
Once a beautiful city to this spoilt state,
The inelegance of the morning,
Skyscrapers, trains, flats and the London Eye,
Open unto the busy roads and to the smoky sky,
All hectic and noisy in the sleepless air,
Never have I seen or felt a fear so deep,
Down below the murky river swarms,
Dear devil, the very flats seem awake,
All that mighty mess lying there.

Robyn James (10)
La Moye School, St Brelade, Jersey

Composed Upon Westminster Bridge
September 3rd 2005

Earth has nothing to show except pure shame
Frightened would he be of soul who could pass by
A sight so disgraceful in its majesty
This city now doth totally unlike a garment wear
The rotten smell in the morning
Loud ships, horrible, ugly towers, big, gloomy domes,
Noisy theatres and temples lie open
Letting out a foul smell into the sky
All dark and grim in the smoky air
Never did the sun shine in the smoke-filled air
The river terrible and rotten
Dear devil! The very houses seem to be awoken
And the whole town is now hideous.

Nathan Hayes (11)
La Moye School, St Brelade, Jersey

Composed Upon Westminster Bridge
September 3rd 2005

Earth has not anything more shameful,
Dull is nobody that sees it,
A gloomy alley in its majesty
Now doth like a garment wear
The diabolical morning; loud and busy
Ships, domes, towers, theatres and temples lie
Open unto the city and to the smoky sky,
All dark and gloomy in the alley
Never did the sun look more devilish and gloomy.

Joshua O'Donoghue (10)
La Moye School, St Brelade, Jersey

Composed Upon Westminster Bridge
September 3rd 2005

Earth has nothing to show that is fair.
A sight so horrid in its majesty,
The city now doth like a garment wear,
The rubbish of the morning noisy and bare,
Boats, trains and billboards lie underground,
With smoke all dull and revolting.
Never did the sun ever shine in the smoky sky,
No valleys, rocks or hills to fill the world.
So angry the River Thames polluted.
Dear devil, the very houses seem woken.
All that mighty rubbish lying there.

Andrew Vallois (10)
La Moye School, St Brelade, Jersey

The School

The bell sounds.
Pupils make their way in.
I am alone for an hour.
Suddenly, I am not.
The pupils come out shouting and screaming.
It's playtime.
They run around without a care in the world.
It's home time.
Everybody tired and out of energy.
Now I can rest.
I am the school.

Jack Hinton (11)
La Moye School, St Brelade, Jersey

Winter

Snow falls down as if I'm crying,
It makes a layer which is my skin,
Santa arrives and jumps into my mouth,
The fire is the heat of my breath,
Christmas time is here with presents and love,
My blood fruity like mulled wine,
Making unachievable resolutions at New Year,
Everything is cold,
For I am Winter.

Katy Hughes (11)
La Moye School, St Brelade, Jersey

Darkness

I destroy the light
My powerful spell making people sleep
I am the ruler of the night
Owls fly from trees into my shadow
Foxes crawl from under me
As I go down, the sun comes up
Now I sleep.

Ben Gibson (10)
La Moye School, St Brelade, Jersey

Christmas

December 25th, for I am Christmas,
Bells jingling all day and night like my golden tonsils,
The wonderful Christmas cooking wafts through my nostrils,
Mistletoe dangling from the tip of my tongue,
Santa has come, presents surrounding me,
My family come and enjoy my bloody wine,
My intestines like the tangled ribbons of presents,
I enjoy the roaring fire.

Kieran Sharman (10)
La Moye School, St Brelade, Jersey

The Blitz

I slam bombs into anything and anyone.
I steal children and fling them into the country.

I paint people's windows with a fine shade of black.
With my great big feet, I kick people into the shelters.

When I approach the city, the sirens fill the air with a deafening sound.
I trash people's lives with one flick.

I am the Blitz.

Kieran Kennedy (10)
La Moye School, St Brelade, Jersey

Lighthouse

I am the lighthouse
My gold light shines off the sea like sunlight
I see ferries, yachts and speedboats sailing by
My tall, thin body is striped red and white
That stands out in the dark night
I think about the ships that have sunk below me
The waves crash to and fro from my feet
My curled stairway leading to the centre of my mind
And the ships shout *ahoy* with their bellowing horns.

Tom Chadd (10)
La Moye School, St Brelade, Jersey

Fear

My heart is full of demons,
Ready to jump out at the next person.
My fingers creep right up your spine.
I blow gusts of wind,
Out of the night sky.
My eyes are red-hot like the sun.
My friend is Scream,
For I am Fear.

James Donnelly (11)
La Moye School, St Brelade, Jersey

The Problem With My Grandad

The problem with my grandad,
Is that he is really crazy.
Once I found him running around the garden,
When it was hazy.

Even though my grandad's kind,
He really, really pongs,
And then I found out,
That he was wearing thongs.

He often goes bonkers
And says he's going out thinking.
But we all think,
He's going out drinking.

He rides around in his Audi,
Thinking he is cool
And then he ends up,
Diving into a pool.

He ended up in hospital,
That was really bad,
But then I found out,
That my grandad was my dad.

No wonder he spent so much time with me,
Having all that fun,
But now the question remains,
Is my grandma my mum?

Jack Treliving (11)
La Moye School, St Brelade, Jersey

The Trouble With My Teacher

The trouble with my teacher:
He loves kangaroos,
He walked into class
Wearing ballet shoes.

He thinks he's a wrestler,
He always beats me up,
I told him,
'Come on, put 'em up.'

Keiffer Davis (10)
La Moye School, St Brelade, Jersey

Limerick

There was a young man from Tashkent,
Who sneezed and blew up his green tent.
He began to feel cold,
On his toes he found mould,
So he buried himself in cement.

Jamie Larbalestier (10)
La Moye School, St Brelade, Jersey

Step By Step

Walking in your footsteps,
Feeling very cold with no shoes or blankets,
Thinking you might die from a cold,
Saying goodbye, I'm going to die.
People trying to help other people make tents
And feeling so sorry
You all have no food or drinks.
You have nowhere to live,
People suffering in the snow.

Aiman Baghiani (8)
Mont Nicolle Primary School, St Brelade, Jersey

Step By Step

We've been walking in your footsteps,
Thinking of you,
You must be feeling so cold
Whilst we are nice and warm.
It must be so hard to get through the thick snow.
We are saying we're sorry for you,
We've been walking in your footsteps.

We've been walking in your footsteps,
Thinking of the snow.
We've been running in your footsteps,
We are thinking of you.
We've been jumping in your footsteps,
Feeling sorry for you.
We've been skipping in your footsteps,
We are on your side.
We've been walking in your footsteps.

Bryony Harris (8) & Nicole Le Cuirot (9)
Mont Nicolle Primary School, St Brelade, Jersey

Ten Things Found In Hagrid's Pocket

A dragon egg, about to hatch any second
Smelly, stinky dog food for his dog, Fang
A diary to list the things that happen on each day
Some weapons to defend himself when he goes in the dark wood
A pair of smelly, dirty, old gardening gloves, size 30
Some smelly, old and battered boots size 50
A book on how to write really neatly
Some quills to write letters with
A book called 'How To Look After Strange Animals'
Some keys that open every room in Hogwarts.

Shea Scott (9)
Mont Nicolle Primary School, St Brelade, Jersey

Ten Things Found In A Busy Mum's Pocket

An old bus ticket to London
A scruffy pink purse
A boring food shopping list
Some loose change
A book about naughty kids and how to make them nice
A packet of travel tissues
A flip-up mobile phone
A bunch of car keys
A silver wedding ring with PD engraved inside
An old-fashioned watch belonging to her granny.

Hannah Taylor (9)
Mont Nicolle Primary School, St Brelade, Jersey

Mum! Mum! Mum!

Mum, they are not there!
Someone has moved them!
My books,
On the table,
Someone's moved them.

Mum, Mum,
It's messy
In my room,
My sisters, they messed up my room,
What shall I do?

Mum, Mum, Mum,
My sisters,
They're being rude
To me,
Can you tell them off?

Eden Harrison (8)
Mont Nicolle Primary School, St Brelade, Jersey

Ten Things Found In Matt Dawson's Pocket

A muddy rugby ball
A worn out rugby boot stud
A gold shiny medal won at the World Cup
A book called 'How To Be A Winning Rugby Player'
A pair of bumpy grip gloves
A silver mobile phone full of team players' numbers
A Union Jack gum shield
A pair of new black shoulder pads
A shirt with number nine on the back
An England flag.

Lauren Lowe (9)
Mont Nicolle Primary School, St Brelade, Jersey

Knight Kennings

Sword-fighter
Horse-rider
Castle-protector
Arrow-shooter
Joust-champion
Armour-wearer
My favourite knight.

Sean Durham-Waite (9)
Mont Nicolle Primary School, St Brelade, Jersey

We Are Talking And Walking With You

We are talking with you.
We are walking in your footsteps.
Wondering how cold the snow is.
We will help you when you need us.

We are talking in your footsteps.
We will come to the rocky mountains.
Through the thick snow
To bring you shoes to last the winter.

Benjamin Carter (8)
Mont Nicolle Primary School, St Brelade, Jersey

Ten Things You Find In A Teacher's Pocket

A little child's toy that she had taken away
A shopping list for tonight's dinner
A paper clip that could come in handy
A packet of smiley stickers
A Fisherman's Friend to clear her throat
A book 'How To Teach Gymnastics'
A mobile phone to phone the head teacher
A whistle for the end of playtime
A key to open the school
A scarf and hat to keep her warm in the playground.

Dominic Ball (8)
Mont Nicolle Primary School, St Brelade, Jersey

Ten Things Found In A Surfer's Pocket

A Billabong hat
A hand towel for when she gets out of the sea
Some surf wax
A book called 'How To Stand Up Without Belly-Flopping Off'
A pair of wetsuit gloves
Fins for different types of surfboards
Sand with some small stones mixed up with the sand
One flip-flop
One big bottle of beer!

Phoebe Gould (9)
Mont Nicolle Primary School, St Brelade, Jersey

What Makes Me Happy

What makes me happy is when I have hot chocolate after school.
What makes me happy is when there's no school.
What makes me happy is when my sister is nice to me.
What makes me happy is when I get to watch TV.
What makes me happy is when I get what I want.
What makes me happy is when you're happy.

Claudia Barker (8)
Mont Nicolle Primary School, St Brelade, Jersey

Mum

Lunch-maker
Toy-buyer
Dinner-cooker
Dish-cleaner
Room-tidier
Bath-runner
Clothes-washer
Bed-maker
Dustbin-filler
Window-cleaner
Floor-sweeper
Best-friend.

Georgia Sharp (8)
Mont Nicolle Primary School, St Brelade, Jersey

Guess Who?

Dog-walker
Pet-brusher
Toy-chooser
Clothes-washer
Food-shopper
Dinner-cooker
Room-tidier
Flower-arranger
Cuddle-giver
My mum!

Cameron O'Neill (8)
Mont Nicolle Primary School, St Brelade, Jersey

Mum! Dad!

Dad! Thomas is getting all my toys out!
Dad! Thomas is putting my doll in his room!

Mum! The cat is eating out of the bin!
Mum! The cat is chewing my coat!

Dad! You said I could watch Scooby-Doo now!
Dad! Thomas is putting my chocolate in the bin!

Mum! The cat ate all Dad's tea!
Mum! I'm going to be late for drama club!

Mum! Dad!
It's not fair!

Sophie Young (8)
Mont Nicolle Primary School, St Brelade, Jersey

Ten Things Found In A Referee's Pocket

A yellow card
A red card
A pencil to write with
A whistle to blow
A handbook of how to book people
A black wristband
A spare league badge
Some Lucozade Sport to drink
Spare red and yellow cards in a waterproof case
A notepad to write in footballers' names.

Max Taylor (8)
Mont Nicolle Primary School, St Brelade, Jersey

When We Both Get Angry . . .

Cassie! Clear up
That mess
Your clothes have been out
For too long!

Cassie! Cassie!
Dinner's ready
Come down now!
It's chicken
Come on! Hurry up!

Cassie! Cassie! Cassie!
You are
Going to
Be *late*
Get down here right now!

Mum - I haven't finished
Tidying my clothes
Give me a chance!

Mum! Mum!
My dinner's burnt!
I'm *not* eating that!
It's black and horrid.

Mum! Mum! Mum!
There's an hour till it's time
To go
Till we need to be there
We've plenty of time.

Cassandra Pickersgill (8)
Mont Nicolle Primary School, St Brelade, Jersey

My Daddy

Football-player
Shed-builder
Toy-fixer
Snack-maker
Thingy-buyer
Pillow-fluffer
Sweetie-buyer
Food-eater
Telly-watcher
Wall-painter . . .

And a Niamhi hugger!

Niamh Martin (9)
Mont Nicolle Primary School, St Brelade, Jersey

Ten Things Found In Ronaldinho's Pocket

Ronaldinho's old pair of football boots
Ronaldinho's old, flat football
A picture of his fancy wife
A pair of really sweaty shin pads
A picture of his old manager
A picture of the stadium and Ronaldinho
A pair of old football socks covered in grass and mud
A box of broken football studs
A soaking piece of turf from Nuo Camp
A pair of old football shorts full of grass stains.

Scott McClurg (8)
Mont Nicolle Primary School, St Brelade, Jersey

Dogs

I wish I had a doggy,
So it would run, jump and play,
I wish I had a doggy,
So I want one right away.

Henry Sayle (9)
Murray's Road Junior School, Douglas, Isle of Man

My Pet

Nibbles, Nibbles, runs around,
Up and down,
Even left and right.
Nibbles chews and chews,
Nibbles, I love you.
He wiggles and wriggles his nose,
The best thing about Nibbles is . . .
He is mine!

Thomas Whitelegg (9)
Murray's Road Junior School, Douglas, Isle of Man

Darkness

At night when the lights go out,
I feel like I want to shout.
It is very dark and lonely
And sometimes I think, if only
I had my own little light,
Then it wouldn't give me such a fright.

Philippa Kennaugh (9)
Murray's Road Junior School, Douglas, Isle of Man

My Kitten

My kitten sleeps anywhere,
She doesn't stare.
She will sleep in a cupboard,
In a basket, on your knee,
And when I call her,
She will come to me.
Miaow!

Emily Rimmer (8)
Murray's Road Junior School, Douglas, Isle of Man

Waking Up On Christmas Day

Waking up on Christmas morning,
Is it today? I think while yawning.
What's at the bottom of my bed?
Excitement buzzes through my head.
I look down at my Santa sacks,
Shapes and sizes, boxes and packs.
Straining my eyes so I can see,
What are they? Presents! All for me!
Suddenly, everyone's awake,
Into Mum's bed our presents we'll take.
Tearing them open one by one,
Christmas Day is so much fun!

Emily Brennan (9)
Murray's Road Junior School, Douglas, Isle of Man

Friends

F riends are forever
R unning round together
I   n all types of weather
E njoying their time whatever
N o arguments ever
D ancing in the heather
S miley faces forever and ever.

Molly Harding (8)
Murray's Road Junior School, Douglas, Isle of Man

Polar Bears

Polar bears have nearly gone
    Only because of global warming
But they are still nearly gone
    Don't cry over it
But they're my favourite animal.

Emma Wilcox (10)
Murray's Road Junior School, Douglas, Isle of Man

I Wish I Had A Pony

I wish I had a pony,
Then I wouldn't be so lonely.
Polo would be his name
And he would have a black mane.
He would live in my shed,
With a comfy bed.
His favourite food would be hay
And his birthday would be in May.
I would take him to school,
It would be so cool.
I wish I had a pony.

Katy Libreri (9)
Murray's Road Junior School, Douglas, Isle of Man

Spring Chicks

Spring chicks are being born,
Spring chicks are walking on the lawn,
Spring chicks are growing up,
Spring chicks are saying goodbye,
'Goodbye, goodbye,' say the spring chicks.

Oops, I forgot . . .
They not spring chicks anymore.

Myriam Raso (9)
Murray's Road Junior School, Douglas, Isle of Man

The Queen

The Queen has a crown
Which sits on her head.

The Queen goes to sleep
In her four-poster bed.

The Queen's favourite food
Is jam and bread.

Jemima Morrow (10)
Murray's Road Junior School, Douglas, Isle of Man

Teacher Tables

'No,' my teacher cried and sighed.
'2 plus 2 must equal 4.'
'But I don't understand this, Miss!
Cos that means 3 plus 3 must equal 6.'
'Now we're getting somewhere, look.
Now you go read your favourite book!'
'No,' I said (I nearly cried),
'But 5 plus 5 equals 55!'
I don't really get this thing,
So now I'm in detention,
Writing . . . writing . . . writing!

Rebecca Johnson (10)
Murray's Road Junior School, Douglas, Isle of Man

The Boy Called Berry

There was a boy called Berry
Who sat on the end of a ferry
The ferry set off and he fell off
And his bum was as red as a cherry.

Jack Berry (11)
Murray's Road Junior School, Douglas, Isle of Man

No!

Can I jump off a cliff? *No!*
Can I swim with sharks? *No!*
Can I go to the shop? *No!*

Do you want to come to the circus? No!

Nicole Burns (8)
Murray's Road Junior School, Douglas, Isle of Man

Why?

'I am going out.'
'Why?'
'Because I'm hungry.'
'Why?'
'Because it's dinner time.'
'Why?'
'Because it's the middle of the day.'
'Why?'
'Why do you keep saying why?'
'What?'

Jamie Kneen (7)
Murray's Road Junior School, Douglas, Isle of Man

Pixies And Fairies

Pixies are small
Fairies are too
They sit on the wall
And admire the view.

Pixies can prance
Fairies can sing
Fairies like to dance
Pixies wish they had wings.

Ella Voysey (9)
Murray's Road Junior School, Douglas, Isle of Man

The Roaring Ocean

Waves crash,
Dolphins splash,
Under the deep blue sea.

Fish swim,
Waving fins,
Under the deep blue sea.

Eleanor Goddard (9)
Murray's Road Junior School, Douglas, Isle of Man

Young Writers - A Pocketful Of Rhyme British Isles

Wildlife

Two little girls,
Sitting on a tree,
One saw a dragonfly,
Another saw a bee.
1, 2, 3,
What do you see?

Eva Boyd (8)
Murray's Road Junior School, Douglas, Isle of Man

Why?

'I am going to see Parker.'
'Why?'
'Cos I want to ride.'
'Why?'
'Cos my friends are.'
'Why?'
'Cos they want to play.'
'Why?'
'Cos I want to go with them.'
'Why?'
'Cos I want to see Parker.'
'Why?'
'Why?'
'Why?'

Katie McKnight (7)
Murray's Road Junior School, Douglas, Isle of Man

Playtime

Lesson out, time to play
Children all have their say
Scream and shout as much as they can
Have to watch out or we'll all get a ban.

Courtney Marchbank (7)
Murray's Road Junior School, Douglas, Isle of Man

My Bestest Friends

I have two bestest friends.

My bestest friend is tall and nearly 10 years old,
Even if she's never been told,
I really like her a lot,
Ever since I was a tot,
My best friend number one is . . .
Emily Mills.

My bestest friend is quite small and has just turned 9,
We get along more than just fine,
We haven't been together for long,
We don't mind if we are wrong.
My best friend number two is . . .
Eleanor Goddard.

Everyone has a good laugh,
Even if we're as different as the length
Of the neck of a giraffe.
I definitely have two bestest friends!

Siobhan Fuller (8)
Murray's Road Junior School, Douglas, Isle of Man

Animals

Dolphins drink, dolphins sleep,
But most of all they like to leap.

Wolves eat, wolves prowl,
But most of all they like to howl.

Cats lick, cats arch,
But most of all they like to march.

Dogs kick, dogs burp,
But most of all they like to slurp.

Fay Wilcox (8)
Murray's Road Junior School, Douglas, Isle of Man

Bullies

There are lots of bullies in this school,
How mean are they?
How keen are they?
They think it's good fun,
But we know it isn't.
We know it's nasty and cruel.

They always tease us when we play.
They think it's cool,
To take our ball,
They think it's a game,
But we know it isn't.
They always bully us every day.

Max Fleurbaay (7)
Murray's Road Junior School, Douglas, Isle of Man

Devils

What are devils? Nobody knows
Could be human, could be clones
Are devils really alive? If they are
How do they survive?
Are devils really real
Or are they just a fairy tale?
Do they always dress in red?
'Are they evil?' someone said
Do they carry big, sharp forks?
Do they always pick on dorks?
Do they all live in Hell
Casting dark, evil spells?

Sam Greasley (8)
Murray's Road Junior School, Douglas, Isle of Man

A Pocket Full Of Rhyme

'What's this?' Mum cried with a shriek,
'I've told you every day - all week,
Sort your pockets - empty them out,
Otherwise I've no choice - just shout!'

I pulled out my hand and showed her the fluff,
String and Blu-tack - all sorts of stuff.
'There's been no time!' I gave a smile,
'I'll sort it out - in a while!'

My mum had asked me to eat my cheese
And then she said, 'Eat your peas!'
But I said, 'No thanks,' and moaned
And hid them while she groaned and groaned.

Along with the cheese and the peas,
There was some honey, which seemed very runny.
'Go to the shop. Here's some money.
Don't look at me as if I'm funny!'
'I'm going! I'm going! Just give me more time,
To sort out the grime in my pocket full of rhyme!'

Caitlin Cowin (8)
Murray's Road Junior School, Douglas, Isle of Man

What?

What do we think?
What do we see?
What do we smell?
What do we taste?
What do we touch?
What do we feel?
What do we fear?
All is not clear!

Owen Phillips (8)
Murray's Road Junior School, Douglas, Isle of Man

Silverdale

Silverdale is a beautiful glen
With boats to sail upon the lake
And a merry-go-round
For the children's sake.

Ice creams from the café
And a picnic on the grass
And while I was there
I saw a girl from my class.

My mum and my brother
And sister came too
To have fun in the park
And say, 'How do you do?'

We can walk by the stream
Right into the glen
To see wild flowers and butterflies
In a lovely place that's always open.

And one day real soon
We will go there again
And hope that our glen
Will still be the same.

Sophie Cuthbert (9)
Murray's Road Junior School, Douglas, Isle of Man

The Boy From Bamboo

There was a boy from Bamboo,
Who went hopping with a kangaroo.
He bounced up too high,
Right into the sky,
That bouncy boy from Bamboo.

Kyle Logan (11)
Murray's Road Junior School, Douglas, Isle of Man

Friends

Friends are who you trust,
Friends are all you need,
Friends will do things that you want,
Friends will give you a feed.

Friends will fight in battles,
Friends may well fall out,
But in my case I think we will all be friends,
Don't you?

India Halsall (9) & Bethanie Christian (8)
Murray's Road Junior School, Douglas, Isle of Man

Teddy Bear

Teddy bear, teddy bear,
You are like an autumn leaf.
Teddy bear, teddy bear,
You are like a cuddly cushion.
Teddy bear, teddy bear,
You are like a soft tissue.

Kelly-Anne Hollingsworth (8)
Murray's Road Junior School, Douglas, Isle of Man

Holiday

My mum and dad and me
Are off on holiday
We are starting off in Manchester
And then the USA
And I'm going to have fun
Yippee!

Charlotte Percival (10)
Murray's Road Junior School, Douglas, Isle of Man

Shakes Of The World

The world shakes with Rayquaza's extreme speed.
The world shakes with Groudon's earthquake.
The sea shakes with Kyogre's sheer cold.
The rocks crumble with Reigirock's super power.
The sky breaks with Salamence's outrage.
The steel crumbles with Beldum's irontail.
The Mount Pyre shakes with Chimecho's psybeam.
The caves crumble with Absol's razorwind.
The codes are cracked with Claydol's earthquake.
The seas are ravaged by Corphish's crabhammer.
The rocky mountains are blazing hot with Camerupt's blastburn.

James Collister (9)
Murray's Road Junior School, Douglas, Isle of Man

There Was A Man From The Mersey

There was a man from the Mersey,
Who wore a great big, red jersey.
He got on the ferry,
To see his friend, Jerry,
That funny old man from the Mersey.

Adam Smith (10)
Murray's Road Junior School, Douglas, Isle of Man

Chocolate!

Chocolate, chocolate, soft and scrummy,
Let it melt inside my tummy.

Belgian, toffee, Pick 'n' mix-mix,
Maltesers, Minstrels and also a Twix.

Although these treats sound so thrilling,
If I'm not careful I'll need a filling.

Katie Banks (11)
Murray's Road Junior School, Douglas, Isle of Man

Fairy, Fairies

Fairies are disgusting things,
They blow bogeys on their wings,
They have green flies in their hair
And have dirty, smelly underwear.

They take your teeth one by one,
In the middle of the night when everyone's gone.
They take them back to fairyland,
To make piano keys for the band.

Everyone thinks that fairies are sweet,
Leaving us money and giving us treats,
But I know something that will make you weep,
Fairies kick you while you sleep.

Ruth Mellon (7)
Murray's Road Junior School, Douglas, Isle of Man

My Best Friend, Rebecca

She's a bright yellow, bouncy chair
She's a tiger jumping for its prey
She's a place in the sun
She's always on the move
She's the sound of birds chirping
She's a morning bowl of cereal
She's an afternoon drink
She's my best friend.

Katherine Blenkinsop (9)
Murray's Road Junior School, Douglas, Isle of Man

Pegasus

The daylight turned to moonlight
The darklight turned to starlight
The jewel is on the wall
It is soon before the moon comes.

Emilia Crocker (6)
St John's School, St John, Jersey

Surfing

Surfing, surfing in the air,
Surfing, surfing in my hair,
Surfing, surfing in the waves,
Surfing, surfing in the caves.
Surfing is wet
And very, very dangerous I bet!
Surfing is scary
And very, very hairy!

Benjamin Tait (6)
St John's School, St John, Jersey

Fairies

Fairies of the night and sky,
Flap their wings and fly.
They climb on the flower,
It gives them so much power.
They must not flitter,
When the rain pitters,
Or the elves,
Will get on the shelves.

Magdalena Thebault (7)
St John's School, St John, Jersey

Fireworks

Fireworks rise like a flying bird.
Each firework unfolds like a bird unfolding his wings.
Catherine wheels begin to flame like a glimmer glitter shine.
Fireworks glitter and shine in the sky!

Hannah Couriard (9)
St John's School, St John, Jersey

The Black Death

The Black Death was gory
And there were fleas and rats.
The fleas bit the rats,
They couldn't take it.

The fleas got carried by the rats,
Through sewers, dungeons, roads and streets.
They spread the plague from south to north,
Killing children and adults too.

The plague started in Italy,
The year 1347.
It ended in Russia,
In 1353.

Kealan Bisson (8)
St John's School, St John, Jersey

The Death Of Beth

There was a girl called Beth,
Who died of the Black Death.
She got it from a rat,
Who'd been caught by her cat.

The doctor tried to cure her,
By sitting her in a sewer.
He also fed her arsenic,
Which he gave her with a long stick.
He then put her in a bed
And drilled a hole in her head.
But that did not work,
Because she went berserk.

Beth had her time,
But it ended in 1349.

Hugh Percival (9)
St John's School, St John, Jersey

As Quick As Animals Can Be

As sly as a fox
As quick as a fox
As swift as a fox
As clever as a fox
That's what I want to be.

As prickly as a hedgehog
As cute as a hedgehog
As slow as a hedgehog
As wise as a hedgehog
That's what I want to be.

As beautiful as a wolf
As smart as a wolf
As slight as a wolf
As strong as a wolf
That's what I want to be.

As quick as animals get
I know I will always be me.

Verity Stanier (8)
St John's School, St John, Jersey

The Electricity Trip

We went on the blue minibus
We sat at the back, both of us.
This was a special trip
To use a crocodile clip.
We had earplugs for the noise
And helmets for girls and boys.
We had to fit the battery
In the black thingy.
When I plug in electricity
It turns on my mum's TV.

Hamish Morrison (6) & Luke Ryan (7)
St John's School, St John, Jersey

My Cats And Me

My cats are the best thing that happened to me.
Fizz is my favourite cat, my cutest cat is Junior.
Thunder is my oldest cat,
Squeaky is my furriest.
Pepsi is my thinnest cat,
But she's still fit.
As I go around,
Thunder follows me wherever I go.
My love for my cats will live forever.

Alexander Le Blancq (9)
St John's School, St John, Jersey

Man U Week

Football is our game
And Man U is our name.
We call for the ball
And we try not to fall.
We play on the pitch
And we run too fast, then we get a stitch.
We like our red Man U kit
Playing football keeps us fit.

Max Cornish (7)
St John's School, St John, Jersey

Fireworks

Fireworks rise like a shooting star bright in the sky.
Each firework unfolds like a bomb going off in 1945 wartime London.
Catherine wheels begin to flame like a blinding flame-thrower.

Shane Galloway (9)
St John's School, St John, Jersey

Moonlight Parade

Howling solves
Dancing racoons
Cooling breeze
Guiding lions
Lonely forests
Living animals
Chilling air
Chilling water.

Áine Loynd (8)
St John's School, St John, Jersey

Fireworks

Fireworks rise
Like bullets in the sky.

Each firework unfolds
Like an egg cracking.

Catherine wheels begin to flame
Like wheels rolling down the hill.

Ben Jehan (9)
St John's School, St John, Jersey

Our Dogs

We have Panzer and Holly,
They're our favourite dogs.
We do not want them to die,
But when they do,
We know they will be happy,
In the sky.

Jake Haslam (9) & Liam Baudin (10)
St John's School, St John, Jersey

Striker Josh

There once was a striker called Josh,
He was very, very posh,
He wore golden boots,
Because the pitch had loads of roots.

The roots were old
And had loads of mould,
Josh was odd,
Because all he did was nod.

Josh, Josh had to go home,
But on the plane,
He stopped at Rome.

Where is Josh?
He had a game,
But he left his kit
On the plane.

Aston Myatt (10)
St John's School, St John, Jersey

Lonely

When I'm lonely
I don't feel down
Because I know
There's someone
Special around.
In the sky
My rabbit awaits
And I know God
Says he's great.
I miss him so
But I know
In my heart
He's still there.

Kelly McCullagh (10)
St John's School, St John, Jersey

My Cat

My cat is very lovely,
She is fun to play with,
She lets me cuddle up to her.
She can be a pest,
But she is also good,
Like the rest.
Puss, puss, you are a good cat.
She likes her family
And she loves me.
She is a very good friend
To have around.
I love my cat
And she loves me.
We're best friends
Until the day she dies.
I love you, pusskins
And you love me.

Catherine Rook (10)
St John's School, St John, Jersey

Tizie And Hazel

Tizie is as white as the clouds that go by,
Up there where the sky is as blue as the sea.
She has spots of black, like coal,
But they are sweet and small
And she has a spot on her nose.
Hazel runs as fast as the wind
And is as gold as golden treacle.
She has black, beady eyes,
That sparkle in the sunlight.
I will always love them,
As much as they love me.

Amy Condron-Dorey (10)
St John's School, St John, Jersey

Life As A Pirate

Land ahoy! I'm going to steal more treasure,
Started this business as a boy,
I could never wish for more pleasure,
Just having a parrot as a toy.

We don't have parents,
We don't need them,
We don't take orders,
For we are young men.

A bottle of rum,
A great big feast,
To fill up my tum,
So that we can sail the east.

Eleisha Rice (9) & Molly Huelin (10)
St John's School, St John, Jersey

A Day In A Hunter's Life!

Howling wolves,
Dancing racoons,
Cooling breeze,
Guiding moonlight,
Lonely forests,
Chilling air,
Living animals,
Chilling water!

Harry Lewis (8)
St John's School, St John, Jersey

Fireworks

Fireworks rise like a wave in the sea.
Each firework unfolds like an umbrella on a windy day.
Catherine wheels begin to flame like a blazing inferno burning on Earth.

Jordan Stott (9)
St John's School, St John, Jersey

Snow

Looking through my window,
Snow is cold and icy, I know.
As I walk through the snow,
It crunches like crystals smashing.
As snowflakes fall,
It looks like they are dancing.
As the sun shines through the icy water,
It looks like little tiny coloured diamonds on top of the water.
When my friends and I walk through the snow,
We make nice patterns with our feet.

Jack McGinney (10)
St John's School, St John, Jersey

My Kitten

My kitten, Amber, is good fun
She likes everyone
She likes food and treats
She loves the sound of drum beats
She is small, she is cute
She is nice, she is cuddly
I love her
She loves me.

Corinne Figueira (9)
St John's School, St John, Jersey

Fireworks

Fireworks rise like a shooting star.
Each firework unfolds like an egg cracking.
Catherine wheels begin to flame like a lion shaking his mane.

Scott Gallichan (8)
St John's School, St John, Jersey

My Family

My parents and I are really precious,
They buy me stuff and I respect them.
I still care about my cat, Tom-Tom,
He is out there somewhere with a new owner,
But I still miss him!
I still have fun even though he's missing.
I have lots of fun when I go out with my family for dinner.
I love them very much!

Ben Bidan (10)
St John's School, St John, Jersey

My Best Friend

You are my best friend
And you always will be,
Today and tomorrow,
Never will I change,
Because you and I
Are best friends
And I know
We will carry on our friendship
Till history ends.

Anya Beuzeval (9)
St John's School, St John, Jersey

Fireworks

Fireworks rise like eggs cracking.
Each firework unfolds like eggs cracking.
Catherine wheels begin to flame like sparks in the air.

Bradley Le Feuvre (8)
St John's School, St John, Jersey

Fireworks

Fireworks rise like a rocket rising to the shining sun.
Each firework unfolds like a tree blossoming in the springtime.
Catherine wheels begin to flame like a motorbike's rear wheel
                                              spinning in the dirt.

Jayson Baudains (8)
St John's School, St John, Jersey

My Dog, Ruby

My dog, Ruby, she is fun,
She makes friends with everyone.
She likes bones, she likes treats,
She likes the sound of drum beats.
She is small, she is cute,
She is nothing like a brute.
She chews slippers, she chews boots,
She slips down the garbage chute.
She is my dog, I love her so,
Look! There she goes!

Chloe McCabe (9)
St John's School, St John, Jersey

When The Wind Blows

When the wind blows
And the sun glows,
Singing goes through the air.
The sound of the singing
Is like whistling
Except no one's there.
When I wish I have a feeling
That I'm going to die,
But day after day,
I'm happy to still be alive.

Claire Le Cornu (9)
St John's School, St John, Jersey

There Are Places And Times For Seasons

There are places and times in this world
For seasons like winter and spring.
Winter snow, hail, sleet and ice, that's winter.
Flowers, leaves, blossom on the trees
And the birds sing in the breeze, that's spring.
Autumn brings the breeze and the leaves, that's autumn.
Summer brings kids from the towns racing to the sea.
There are places and times for seasons.

Philip Mitchell (10)
St John's School, St John, Jersey

My Family

My family are my life,
My family are my death,
My family can help me through life,
They help me when I'm sick or hurt,
I love my family, they love me,
I wish they would never die.

Robyn Nerac (9)
St John's School, St John, Jersey

My Glass Music Box

The light reflects in my eye
And sparkles and glitters on my mantelpiece.
My glass music box is always there,
Through the bad times.
A gift from Granny,
The greatest gift she has given.
I shall keep it forever, my music box!

Alexander Touzel (10)
St John's School, St John, Jersey

My Dog

Teddy is a dog,
He always jumps at my feet,
He barks all the time,
He likes going to the beach.

But he doesn't like going on the road,
He likes having chocolates,
He also likes licking things
And he looks like a lion.

Jack Lewis (9)
St John's School, St John, Jersey

My Family

My family is my light.
They give me what I need.
I receive rest when I need it
And they are my saviours.
They guide me through the dark forest.
They never do any sins.
My dad watches the football
And hopes Man U win.

Alex Watson (10)
St John's School, St John, Jersey

My Family!

My family, they give me a heartful of respect
They give me everything I need and like
They let me go to France and the UK
They love me very much and always look out for me
My family.

George Queree (9)
St John's School, St John, Jersey

My Little Winter World!

The snow on the trees is like tinsel,
The pointy, sharp icicles are like frozen glass,
The snowflakes dancing in the air around me,
In this wonderful winter world.

The shimmering blanket of snow looks like ice cream,
The crunching snow under your feet,
The dusting layer of snow,
In this wonderful winter world.

As I go indoors from the winter world,
I go into my cosy bed
And remember,
My little winter world.

Jessica Stamps (11)
St John's School, St John, Jersey

Winter World

Winter is an icy cold, silent world,
Where most sound is blocked out
By the gentle melody of falling snow
And the dripping of icicles
Melting in the mellow sun.

The pond shatters
As I throw a stone on its surface.
Winter is cold, winter is icy,
Winter is here.

Rikki Beuzeval (11)
St John's School, St John, Jersey

Outside In The Snow

Outside in the snow,
Snowflakes swirling and diving around me,
Creating an Arctic world.
The next morning the sun glittering,
On the icy blanket of snow,
Bare trees are dark silhouettes
Against the wintry sky
And when the freezing cold
Reaches my toes through my boots,
I go inside,
Take off my boots, my scarf, my gloves, my coat
And sit down in front of a glowing fire,
With a slice of warm apple pie.

Nadia Crocker (10)
St John's School, St John, Jersey

Winter Land Recipe

Put in a slab of freezing ice that sparkles,
Then add a million glistening snowflakes
With some powdery snow.

Next, add your mystical, crystal paradise,
Add a dusting of snowfrost to make it whiten,
Then add your dark, mucky trees
With a sprinkle of sunlight.

Put in a very cold and frosty place at -10°
For twenty-four hours.
When frosted, add an icicle snowman.
Eat within three months or *melt down!*

Bradley Delap (10)
St John's School, St John, Jersey

Winter Is Here!

As I walk through the crunchy blanket of snow,
I see the trees bare and cold.
The sun shimmers over the white page, that is the ground,
This Arctic world is magical, but freezing.
In my house I feel warm and safe,
But outside there is a new world to be discovered.
The snowflakes dance and swirl all around me,
I make patterns with my footprints and say goodbye as I leave them.
The howling wind, the bright blue sky,
It's wet and cold, but my clothes keep me warm and dry.

Emma Nelson (10)
St John's School, St John, Jersey

Frosty Nights

The dark, sacred nights,
Are here again.
I sit right in front of the fire.
I've hung my decorations,
They are the nicest things I have ever seen!

Why can't it be Christmas all year?

I run outside and see a bird,
A magpie - it is all alone.
The snow is cold and frosty,
The shiny, bright winter moonlight,
The white crystals of the snowflakes,
But Mummy calls me in.

Jarina Le Main (10)
St John's School, St John, Jersey

Winter Wonderland

Icicles hanging,
Snowflakes falling,
So there's no school on a Monday morning!

Trees are bare,
Snow is frozen,
A magical world is just appearing.

Frosty, sparkling Arctic world,
Icy, freezing, howling wind,
Snowflakes dancing in the air.

Paige Therin (11)
St John's School, St John, Jersey

Snow

Snow is freezing, icy and white,
Snow is shiny, soft and powdery,
Snow is mystical, magical and glossy.

Snow is falling from the winter-grey sky,
Snow is dancing, floating and swirling down,
Snow is stationary on the trees.

Peter Rondel (10)
St John's School, St John, Jersey

Winter

Winter
A cold, frosted three months.
Snowflakes with six points
Fall from the sky.
Everything white and freezing
Like a polar bear.
All the trees lose their leaves
Except for the evergreens.

Matthew Palmer (9)
St Peter's Primary School, St Peter, Jersey

Severe Winter

I was in my bed
And I was asleep in my cosy pyjamas
A severe winter was ahead.

When I got up
Mum's car wouldn't start
The head teacher said, 'School's out!'

I played with my friends
Having a snowball fight
My hands were cold.

I had to go inside
Because my hands were numb
But I'd had my fun this winter.

Sam Gorvel (8)
St Peter's Primary School, St Peter, Jersey

Real December Night

When I woke up on Christmas Eve
It was hailing strong
So I couldn't go out.
Food lay on the table
Lights flickered outside from other houses
Christmas cake with icing on
Waiting to be eaten.
Frost lay thick with snow
On the ground.
Children shouted, 'Hooray!'
For the beautiful presents.

Amir Ben-Romdhane (9)
St Peter's Primary School, St Peter, Jersey

Snow

It lands quietly on the ground
Like a white cake,
It covers the trees with icing sugar,
Frosty bites nip your face,
Ice crunches under your feet,
A fluffy coat in your hair and
The houses disappear under a blanket.
I slip and slide down big hills,
Snowballs sting my head
And the water dribbles down my back.
When you walk through the snow,
It's like sinking in the sand,
When you walk through the door,
Your hands burn like fire.

Emmanuelle Belligoi (8)
St Peter's Primary School, St Peter, Jersey

My Dinosaur

My dinosaur is vicious
You'd better watch out
He might be lurking behind you
My dinosaur is not like any other dinosaur
You'd better watch out
He might bite you
If you're not aware
My dinosaur is strong
If he smells danger
He brings out his claws.

Alex De La Perrelle (9)
St Peter's Primary School, St Peter, Jersey

My Favourite Food

Dolmio is the best,
When I have some,
I want the rest!
And I hope it isn't
From the west!

Candy sticks are so delicious,
The man who brings them
Is so suspicious.
That's what makes them
So nutritious!

Roast potatoes are nice and crispy,
And on the inside
They're soft and wispy!
My dad serves them,
With lashings of gravy,
I think he could be
A cook in the Navy!

Ice creams are very cold,
The man who serves them
Is very bold!
And my favourite one,
Looks like gold.
That's the one
That I almost sold!

And that is the end
Of the perfect dish,
Even though,
I forgot the fish!

Sophie Wolstenholme (8)
St Peter's Primary School, St Peter, Jersey

Robin Sings

One winter morning
The robins were singing
Their beautiful song.
I heard the *tweet, tweet, tweet*
Which they sung.
They were singing 'Merry Christmas'.
They were in great tune,
I did not want to shut my window.

It was starting to snow,
The robins were still singing,
Tweet, tweet, tweet,
That beautiful tune.
It was so good,
I did not want to close my window.

Rebecca Knight (9)
St Peter's Primary School, St Peter, Jersey

Snow Winter

The snow ran down
And made the ground all hard and white.
All of the animals go
Back to their nests
And rest.

Load the snow and
Make a ball and fight
When you like.
The trees and leaves go
Bright and white.
Hail falls and breaks the walls.

Leo Loftsson (9)
St Peter's Primary School, St Peter, Jersey

A Nice Little Man

Before I went to bed
Mum called me and said
'This is a special night
So pull your cover tight.

A little man will come
Down our chimney tall
Waiting, waiting for you to fall asleep
Making sure no one takes your heap.

He goes around the world
Where children fall asleep
Waiting for this little man
To make a lovely heap.

And this man is called
Santa Claus!'

Sophia Martins (8)
St Peter's Primary School, St Peter, Jersey

Xmas Is Coming

Xmas is coming
The winter robin is singing
In the winter snow.
It's the best season to be happy
Because Christmas is nearly here.

As Santa rides on his sleigh
And passes the singing robin,
Giving presents around the world
As children fall asleep.

Abby McLaughlin (9)
St Peter's Primary School, St Peter, Jersey

The Silent Night Sky

Frosty wind blows by,
In a grey winter sky.
Fairy whizzes past,
More snow at last.
The frozen icy wind,
Goes through the wild whistling.

Stars shoot as fast as Santa,
Reindeer pull his sleigh.
The red nose guides it,
As they're in the grey night sky.
West and east he travels,
Further and further they go,
Through the silent night sky.

Joshua Benest (8)
St Peter's Primary School, St Peter, Jersey

My Horse

Horses are sweet,
Horses are fun,
Horses are handy to go for a run.

Horses are pretty,
But mine's the prettiest of them all,
For his name is Lucky.

We enter a jumping competition,
People cheer from all around,
It's time to jump up to the sky
And then I come home with a red rosette.

Kayleigh Nield (8)
St Peter's Primary School, St Peter, Jersey

My Baby Bunnies

My baby bunnies
Are a bundle of fun,
They are cute and cuddly
And certainly not dumb.

Their eyes are bright
Like a gleaming light,
That flashes in the dark
Like a beautiful spark.

They are cheeky little bunnies
I don't doubt that,
But one thing's for sure
They light up my life.

My baby bunnies
Are now big, strong rabbits,
And they especially like
To eat all the carrots.

Deborah Le Rendu (9)
St Peter's Primary School, St Peter, Jersey

Mr Jack Frost

Jack Frost came last night
And made our garden white,
Then off he flew to some place new
And left us with a stunning sight.

But out came the sun
And melted tons and tons
Of what I think was snow.

Now we can see a daffodil,
Spring is here, we can play
And Jack Frost has flown away.

Esther Le Ruez (9)
St Peter's Primary School, St Peter, Jersey

Poor Old Mrs Edwards

Poor old Mrs Edwards,
It was 1963,
Tried and tried with all her might
And prayed for sun would she.

Her mum would make hot chocolate,
In a big silver blister,
But then she'd look out of the window
And then faint at the sight of a twister!

She stomped up the stairs with anger,
And got into her bed,
But then she had a nasty shock
And fell out of bed!

If I saw an unluckier person,
I'd have to write a book,
I'd sell ten million copies,
For the nation to look at . . .

Poor old Mrs Edwards,
It was 1963,
Tried and tried with all her might
And prayed for sun would she!

Daniel MacFarlane (9)
St Peter's Primary School, St Peter, Jersey

Dinosaurs

Dinosaurs are big
And they have big feet.
Sometimes if you touch them,
They can bite you.
They can eat you,
They run fast.
They have big tails,
They can smash you.

João Sousa (8)
St Peter's Primary School, St Peter, Jersey

Summer Day

The sun was shining at early dawn,
The birds were singing their songs,
Just a few people were getting up to go to the beach,
It was looking as if it was going to be a lovely day.
The children were jumping up and down with excitement,
To make lots of sandcastles on the golden sands
And to go in the sea with the big waves knocking them over.

Lauren Handscomb (9)
St Peter's Primary School, St Peter, Jersey

Summer

I like summer because I can dance,
Summer is so nice, I can prance,
I can run around in my garden,
Doing cartwheels and handstands,
Eating fruit and chocolate,
So how wonderful summer is,
But in the winter you cannot do anything,
How wonderful summer is
I can't wait for summer to come round again.

Ashley Knights (8)
St Peter's Primary School, St Peter, Jersey

Cold Sea

It was windy on a cold, cold day
And the sea was frozen like a snowman.
The wind felt like an ice cube
And boats were struggling to land.
People ran to their homes,
Fishermen returned from the sea,
No fishing, under ice.
Dark nights, everybody lit their fires.

Luke Oughton (9)
St Peter's Primary School, St Peter, Jersey

Winter Morning

I was on my bed sleeping and I heard a bang on my window.
I looked out and there were snowballs hitting my window.
I shouted out, 'It's snowing on our windows!'
I went outside and saw white everywhere.
I saw snowflakes falling from the sky.
I went to get my skis out.
I ran down the big hill and skidded at the bottom.
I climbed back up
And skied down again.
Snowflakes shaped like stars still fell from the sky.
I was too cold so I returned to the warmth of my house.

Daniel McMillan (9)
St Peter's Primary School, St Peter, Jersey

Winter Day

Children building snowmen
Walking through the snow
The frosted river stops their flow.

Angels in the snow
Children getting tired
Now it's time to lay your head
In your warm and cosy bed.

James Wall (9)
St Peter's Primary School, St Peter, Jersey

Snow

The snow is here
The snow is here
The snowmen are playing football
School is out and the snow is falling
So be good because Santa
Is coming to town.

Bradley Le Couteur (8)
St Peter's Primary School, St Peter, Jersey

The Spell

The spell of a white quilt
Which covered the world,
Like a cream pudding in space,
Which reminds us of Christmas
And a man in a red suit.
Gives presents to all good children,
Drums, dolls, toy ships and a wooden man,
To children of young age,
To be happy all year until the next.

Feathers of geese and birds clucking,
Out in the dark sky of full moon,
On the night of Christmas Day.
The man in the red suit,
Whose name is quite cold,
For cold days and cold nights.
Santa Claus or Father Christmas
Can be his name
And reindeer to pull his sleigh.

Rafael Pires (9)
St Peter's Primary School, St Peter, Jersey

Christmas Eve

I sleep inside my snuggly bed
Holding onto my ted
I hold my pillow over my head
And I snuggle up to my ted.

I hear the family singing carols
Wrapped up warm on Christmas Eve
I go to bed to wait for Santa
In the morning I open my presents
Fast as a shot
I get what I asked for
I am as happy as ever.

Kai Walters (8)
St Peter's Primary School, St Peter, Jersey

I Love To Dance

I love to dance
And show off my moves,
Jump up and down
And get in my groove.

I love to dance
And be on stage
Maybe in a show
Or a big parade.

I love to dance
Dancing is fun,
Dancing is cool
It's for everyone!

Sophie Franckel (9)
St Peter's Primary School, St Peter, Jersey

Bullies

I really don't like bullies
They make me really mad
Picking on the little kids
And making them sad

It happens in the playground
It happens in the cloakroom
And it is really cruel

I wish that it would stop
And everyone was happy
Like all the children in my school
Who are kind and very generous.

Megan Ward (8)
St Peter's Primary School, St Peter, Jersey

Waiting!

As I wait for traffic
I also wait for post
I wait for excitement
But for you I wait the most.

I can't wait to see your tiny fingers and toes
And kiss your button nose
I often sit and wonder
Who you'll look like the most.

Whilst I wait for you
I sit in your bedroom
All decorated brand new
The day is getting nearer
And the thought of meeting you more clearer.

You are due to arrive
When the flowers come out in spring
The thought of holding you
Is a wonderful thing
My newborn baby brother
All dressed in blue
With my love from me to you.

Lisa Saout (9)
St Peter's Primary School, St Peter, Jersey